Weathering

Books by Alastair Reid

POETRY
To Lighten My House
Oddments Inklings Omens Moments
Passwords
Weathering

PROSE
Passwords: Places, Poems, Preoccupations
Hispanics (forthcoming)

WORD BOOK
Ounce Dice Trice

FOR CHILDREN
I Will Tell You of a Town
Fairwater
Allth
Supposing
A Balloon for a Blunderbuss
To Be Alive

TRANSLATION
Pablo Neruda: *We Are Many*
Pablo Neruda: *Extravagaria*
Pablo Neruda: *Fully Empowered*
Pablo Neruda: *Selected Poems* (part-translator)
Pablo Neruda: *A New Decade* (with Ben Belitt)
Pablo Neruda: *Isla Negra* (forthcoming)
Jorge Luis Borges: *The Gold of the Tigers*
Jorge Luis Borges: *Ficciones* (part-translator)
Jorge Luis Borges: *A Personal Anthology* (part-translator)
Jorge Luis Borges: *Selected Poems* (part-translator)
José Emilio Pacheco: *Don't Ask Me How the Time Goes Past*

Into Spanish
Mother Goose in Spanish (with Anthony Kerrigan)

WEATHERING

Poems and Translations

ALASTAIR REID

CANONGATE

First published in 1978
by Canongate Publishing Ltd
17 *Jeffrey Street, Edinburgh*

© Alastair Reid 1953, 1959, 1960, 1963, 1964, 1965, 1966, 1967, 1968, 1969, 1970, 1971, 1972, 1973, 1974, 1975, 1976, 1977. © this collection, 1978

ISBN 0 903937 29 8 Hardback
0 903937 30 1 Paperback

Designed by Ruari McLean
Printed and bound in Great Britain
by Robert MacLehose & Co. Ltd
Printers to the University of Glasgow

Contents

Collections of poems, with their parenthetical dates, have something of the aura of tombstones; but, for a poet, the main point in publishing them is to set the poems free, like grown children, in order to turn, unencumbered, to the blank page of the present.

The poems in this volume include some from my three previous books—*To Lighten My House*, 1953, *Oddments Inklings Omens Moments*, 1959, and *Passwords*, 1963, all out of print—which seem to deserve a continuing existence, along with a number of new poems which, although they have been aired in magazines, have never been gathered together. The whole collection spans some twenty-five years.

Some acknowledgments are due: to *The New Yorker*, where most of the poems have appeared, to *The Atlantic Monthly*, *The Listener*, *Encounter*, and *Delos*.

I have included a handful of translations from various volumes, which I feel can stand on their own as English poems; and I should like to acknowledge the generosity of various publishers—Jonathan Cape, Delacorte Press, Farrar, Straus & Giroux, Grove Press, Penguin Books, and Souvenir Press—in granting me permission to reproduce them.

I look on this book as something of a farewell on my part to formal poetry, which seems to me now something of an artificial gesture, like wearing a tie. I am more interested in the essential act of putting-well-into-words, good writing; and I feel that the fine attention one gives to words in poems can also be applied to prose. But it is from poetry more than anything that one learns to say well.

Alastair Reid

In memory of
five generous friends
and moving spirits

MAX AUB 1903–1972
RICHARD F. C. HULL 1913–1974
VICTOR PROETZ 1897–1966
WILLIAM ARNOLD REID 1890–1975
MARC SLONIM 1894–1976

and always
for my dear
K. S. D.

I

Growing, Flying, Happening

Say the soft bird's name, but do not be surprised
to see it fall
headlong, struck skyless, into its pigeonhole—
columba palumbus and you have it dead,
wedged, neat, unwinged in your head.

That that black-backed tatter-winged thing
straking the harbour water and then plummeting
down, to come up, sleek head a-cock,
a minted herring shining in its beak,
is a *guillemot*, is neither here nor there
in the amazement of its rising,
wings slicing the stiff salt air.

That of that spindling spear-leaved plant,
wearing the palest purple umbel,
many-headed, blue-tinted, stilt-stalked
at the stream-edge, one should say briefly
angelica, is by-the-way (though grant
the name itself to be beautiful).
Grant too that any name
makes its own music, that *bryony*, *sally-my-handsome*
burst at their sound into flower,
and that *falcon* and *phalarope* fly off in the ear,
still,
names are for saying at home.

The point is seeing—the grace
beyond recognition, the ways
of the bird rising, unnamed, unknown,
beyond the range of language, beyond its noun.
Eyes open on growing, flying, happening,

3

and go on opening. Manifold, the world
dawns on unrecognising, realising eyes.
Amazement is the thing.
Not love, but the astonishment of loving.

Oddments, Inklings, Omens, Moments

Oddments, as when
you see through skin,
when flowers appear
to be eavesdropping,
or music somewhere
declares your mood;
when sleep fulfils
a feel of dying
or fear makes ghosts
of clothes on a chair.

Inklings, as when
some room rhymes
with a lost time,
or a book reads
like a well-known dream;
when a smell recalls
portraits, funerals,
when a wish happens
or a mirror sees
through distances.

Omens, as when
a shadow from nowhere
falls on a wall,
when a bird seems
to mimic your name,
when a cat eyes you
as though it knew
or, heavy with augury,
a crow caws
cras cras from a tree.

Moments, as when
the air's awareness
makes guesses true,
when a hand's touch
speaks past speech
or when, in poise,
two sympathies
lighten each other,
and love occurs
like song, like weather.

Was, Is, Will Be

It was to have been
an enchanted spring—
the house friendly,
the neighbours kindly,
the mornings misted,
the birds soft-breasted,
the children easy,
the days lazy
with early flowers,
the time, ours.

Not as it is—
days ill-at-ease,
a plague of crows,
the first leaves slow,
the children jumpy,
the cook skimpy,
slant rain in streams,
goblin dreams,
the roof leaky,
work unlikely.

Or will be later
when, like a dead letter,
the past stiffens
and afterthought softens.
Yet, distant in winter,
I still will wonder—
was it we who engendered
the spring's condition,
or a ghost we had angered
with expectation?

Directions for a Map

Birds' eyes see almost this, a tiny island
odd as a footprint on a painted sea.
But maps set margins. Here, the land is measured,
changed to a flat, explicit world of names.

Crossing the threads of roads to nibbled coastlines,
the rivers run in veins that crack the surface.
Mountains are dark like hair, and here and there
lakes gape like moth holes with the sea showing through.

Between the seaports stutter dotted shiplines,
crossing designs of latitude and language.
The towns are flying names. The sea is titled.
A compass crowns the corner like a seal.

Distance is spelt in alphabets and numbers.
Arrows occur at intervals of inches.
There are no signs for love or trouble, only
dots for a village and a cross for churches.

Here space is free for once from time and weather.
The sea has pause. To plot is possible.
Given detachment and a careful angle,
all destinations are predictable.

And given, too, the confidence of distance,
strangers may take a hundred mural journeys.
For once the paths are permanent, the colours
outlast the seasons and the deaths of friends.

And even though, on any printed landscape,
directions never tell you where to go,
maps are an evening comfort to the traveller—
a pencil line will quickly take him home.

The Waterglass

A church tower crowned the town,
double in air and water,
and over anchored houses
the round bells rolled at noon.
Bubbles rolled to the surface.
The drowning bells swirled down.

The sun burned in the bay.
A lighthouse towered downward,
moored in mirroring fathoms.
The seaweed swayed its tree.
The boat below me floated
upside down on the sky.

An underwater wind
ruffled the red-roofed shallows
where wading stilt-legged children
stood in the clouded sand,
and down from the knee-deep harbour
a ladder led to the drowned.

Gulls fell out of the day.
The thrown net met its image
in the window of the water.
A ripple slurred the sky.
My hand swam up to meet me,
and I met myself in the sea.

Mirrored, I saw my face
in the underworld of the water,
and saw my drowned self sway in
the glass day underneath—
till I spoke to my speaking likeness,
and the moment broke with my breath.

The Rain in Spain

Unmediterranean
today, the punctual sun
sulks and stays in

and heavily down the mountain
across olive and pine
rolls a scrim of rain.

Faces press to windows.
Strangers moon and booze.
Innkeepers doze.

Slow lopsided clocks
tick away weeks.
Rudely the weather knocks

and starts up old ills,
insect-itch, boils.
The mail brings bills.

Lovers in their houses
quarrel and make promises
or, restless, dream of cities.

Ghosts in the rafters mutter.
Goats grunt and clatter.
Birds augur water.

The Swiss poet is sick.
The postman kicks his dog.
Death overtakes a pig.

Books turn damp and sour.
Thunder grumbles somewhere.
Sleepers groan in nightmare,

each sure that the sky teems
with his personal phantoms,
each doomed to his own bad dreams.

For who is weather-wise
enough to recognise
which ills are the day's, which his?

Once at Piertarvit

Once at Piertarvit,
one day in April,
the edge of spring,
with the air a-ripple
and sea like knitting,
as Avril and Ann
and Ian and I
walked in the wind
along the headland,
Ian threw an apple
high over Piertarvit.

Not a great throw,
you would say, if you'd seen it,
but good for Ian.
His body tautened,
his arm let go
like a flesh-and-bone bow,
and the hard brown apple
left over from autumn
flew up and up,
crossing our gaze,
from the cliff at Piertarvit.

Then all at once, horror
glanced off our eyes,
Ann's, mine, Avril's.
As the apple curved
in the stippled sky,
at the top of its arc,
it suddenly struck
the shape of a bird,
a gull that had glided
down from nowhere
above Piertarvit.

We imagined the thud
and the thin ribs breaking,
blood, and the bird
hurtling downwards.
No such thing.
The broad wings wavered
a moment only,
then air sustained them.
The gull glided on
while the apple fell
in the sea at Piertarvit.

Nobody spoke.
Nobody whistled.
In that one moment,
our world had shifted.
The four of us stood
stock-still with awe
till, breaking the spell,
Ian walked away
with a whirl in his head.
The whole sky curdled
over Piertarvit.

I followed slowly,
with Ann and Avril
trailing behind.
We had lost our lightness.
Even today,
old as I am,
I find it hard
to say, without wonder,
"Ian hit a bird
with an apple, in April,
once at Piertarvit."

The Tale the Hermit Told

It was one afternoon when I was young
in a village near here, which no one now remembers—
why, I will tell you—an afternoon of fiesta,
with the bells of the hermitage echoing in the mountains,
and a buzz of voices, and dogs barking. Some said
it could all be heard as far as Calatayud.
I was a boy then, though at that perilous point
when tiny things could terrify and amaze me.
The dust in the village square had been watered down,
and we waited, laughing and jostling
the satin rumps of the gypsy dancers.
Across from us, the girls, all lace and frills,
fluttered like tissue paper. Then at a signal,
as the charcoal-burner's dog rolled over and over,
shedding its ribbons, the village band
blundered into tune, and the day began.

    The dancing dizzied me. There was one gypsy
unlike the others, tall, who spun on her feet,
laughing to herself, lost in her own amazement.
I watched her as though in a dream. All round,
my uncles and other men were calling *olé*
while the women tittered and pouted.
There were more feet than shoes, more wine than glasses,
and more kisses than lips. The sun was burning.
Next came a magician, an ugly sly-eyed man
not from our district. "Fiesta, fiesta" he called,
then, chanting a kind of spell, he swore
he would conjure a live dove out of the air.
I saw the dove's wing peeping from his pocket,
so I wandered away, hating the sound of him,
among the tables, heavy with food and wine.
And there was the gypsy girl, standing alone,
head turned away to listen, as though she heard

bells in the hills. She saw me, and her eyes,
which were azure, not black, mocked me.
I could not stop looking. Lightly she danced across
and, keeping her eyes on mine, poured out
a glass of golden wine, and put it before me.
      I glanced from her eyes to the wine. In it, the sun
was a small gold coin, the people looked like nuts.
The band were brass buttons, the towering mountains
the size of pebbles, the houses matchboxes
about the thumbnail square. A miniature magician
was letting loose a dove, which floated upwards,
and there, in that golden, glass-held afternoon,
were those mocking eyes. Time in that moment hung
upside down. In a gulp, I drank the wine.
      What happened next? You must listen.
Goggling boys, girls, dogs, band, gypsies, village,
dove, magician, all rolled down my throat.
Even the music glugged once and was gone.
I was standing nowhere, horrified, alone,
waiting for her eyes to appear and laugh
the afternoon back, but nothing moved or happened.
Nothing, nothing, nothing.
      All that night, I lay in a clump of pines
and seemed to hear the hunters with their dogs
(unribboned now) closing to flush me out.
I hid my face in the needles. All the next day,
I tried to wish the village back, to vomit
the wine, to free the white dove and the music.
I could not. And as time passed,
I lived on bitter nuts and bark and grasses,
and grew used to the woods. I am still here
on this barren mountainside. The years are nothing.
      Yet I am sure of this—
that somewhere in my body there is fiesta,
with ribboned dogs, balloons, and children dancing
in a lost village, that only I remember.

14

Often I have visions, and I hear
voices I know call out. Was it the false magician
who tempted me to magic? Or was it
the gypsy girl who dropped her eyes in a glass
and asked me to work wonders?
Even now, in age, I wait to see her,
still a girl, come spiralling through the woods,
bringing her mystery to me, and with her eyes
teaching me to undream myself, and be
a boy again, believing in a dove
made out of air, that circles overhead
on a lost afternoon of fiesta.

A Game of Glass

I do not believe this room
with its cat and its chandelier,
its chessboard-tiled floor,
its shutters that open out
on an angel playing a fountain,
and the striped light slivering in
to a room that looks the same
in the mirror over my shoulder,
with a second glass-eyed cat.

15

My book does not look real.
The room and the mirror seem
to be playing a waiting game.
The cat has made its move,
the fountain has one to play,
and the thousand eyes of the angel
in the chandelier above
gleam beadily, and say
the next move is up to me.

How can I trust my luck?
Whatever way I look,
I cannot tell which is the door,
and I do not know who is who—
the thin man in the mirror
or the watery one in the fountain.
The cat is eyeing my book.
What am I meant to do?
Which side is the mirror on?

The Manse

The house that shored my childhood up
razed to the ground? I stood, amazed,
gawking at a block of air,
unremarkable except
I had hung it once with crazy
daywish and nightmare.

Expecting to pass a wistful
indulgent morning, I had sprung the gate.
Facing me was a wood
between which and myself
a whole crow-gabled and slated
mythology should have stood.

No room now for the rambling
wry remembering I had planned;
nor could I replant
that plot with a second childhood.
Luck, to have been handed
instead a forgettable element,

and not to have had to meet
regretful ghosts in rooms of glass.
That house by now is fairytale
and I can gloss it over
as easily as passing
clear through a wall.

My Father, Dying

At summer's succulent end,
the house is green-stained.
I reach for my father's hand

and study his ancient nails.
Feeble-bodied, yet at intervals
a sweetness appears and prevails.

The heavy-scented night
seems to get at his throat.
It is as if the dark coughed.

In the other rooms of the house,
the furniture stands mumchance.
Age has engraved his face.

Cradling his wagged-out chin,
I shave him, feeling bone
stretching the waxed skin.

By his bed, the newspaper lies furled.
He has grown too old
to unfold the world,

which has dwindled to the size of a sheet.
His room has a stillness to it.
I do not call it waiting, but I wait,

anxious in the dark, to see if
the butterfly of his breath
has fluttered clear of death.

There is so much might be said,
dear old man, before I find you dead;
but we have become too separate

now in human time
to unravel all the interim
as your memory goes numb.

But there is no need for you to tell—
no words, no wise counsel,
no talk of dying well.

We have become mostly hands
and voices in your understanding.
The whole household is pending.

I am not ready
to be without your frail and wasted body,
your miscellaneous mind-way,

the faltering vein of your life.
Each evening, I am loth
to leave you to your death.

Nor will I dwell on
the endless, cumulative question
I ask, being your son.

But on any one
of these nights soon,
for you, the dark will not crack with dawn,

and then I will begin
with you that hesitant conversation
going on and on and on.

II

For Her Sake

Her world is all aware. She reads
omens in small happenings, the fall of a teaspoon,
flurries of birds, a cat's back arching,
words unspoken, wine spilt.
She will notice moods in handwriting,
be tuned to feelings in a room,
sense ill luck in a house, take heed of ghosts,
hear children cry before the sound has reached her,
stay unperturbed in storms, keep silence
where speech would spoil. Days are her changes,
weather her time.

Whether it be becalmed in cool mornings
of air and water, or thunderstruck through nights
where flesh craves and is answered, in her, love
knows no division, is an incarnation
of all her wonder, as she makes
madness subside, and all thought-splintered things
grow whole again.

Look below. She walks in the garden,
preoccupied with paths, head bent,
beautiful, not at rest, as objects are,
but moving, in the fleck of light and shade.
Her ways are hers, not mine. Pointless to make
my sense of her, or claim her faithfulness.
She is as women are, aware
of her own mystery, in her way faithful
to flowers and days; and from the window's distance,
I watch her, haunted by her otherness.

Well to love true women, whose whims are wise,
whose world is warm, whose home is time,

and well to pleasure them, since, last of all,
they are the truth which men must tell,
and in their pleasure, houses lighten,
gardens grow fruitful, and true tales are told.
Well to move from mind's distance
into their aura, where the air
is shifting, intimate, particular.

And of true women, she, whose eyes illumine
this day I wake in—well to mark
her weather, how her look is candid,
her voice clear-toned, her heart private,
her love both wild and reticent.
Well to praise and please her, well to make
this for her sake.

In Such a Poise is Love

Why should a hint of winter
shadow the window while the insects enter,
or a feel of snowfall, taking corners off
the rough wall and the roof,
while the sun, hanging in the sky,
hotly denies its contrary?

As if it knew all future must entail
probable tempered by improbable,
so the mind wanders to the unforeseen,
and the eye, waking, poises between
shock and recognition—the clothes, the chair,
bewildering, familiar.

In such a poise is love. But who
can keep the balance true,
can stay in the day's surprise, moving
between twin fears, of losing and of having?
Who has not, in love's fever,
insisted on the fatal vow, "for ever,"
and sensed, before the words are gone,
the doom in them dawn?

For Ring-Givers

Given the gift of a ring,
what circle does it close?
What does it say, passing
from lover to lover?
That love, encircled so,
rings for ever?

Or is it the round of love?
Does the ring say
"So must love move,
and in its altering weather,
you two will turn away
as now you turn together"?

Is the ring given or lent?
Does love ring round us
or do we ring round it?
Ring-giver, be warned.
Are you, in turn, expecting
love or the ring returned?

A Lesson for Beautiful Women

Gazing and gazing in the glass,
she might have noticed slow cotillions pass
and might have seen
a blur of others in the antique green.
Transfixed instead,
she learned the inclinations of her neat small head
and, startling her own surprise,
wondered at the wonder in her jewelled eyes.

Gardens of rainbow and russet might have caught her
but, leaning over goldfish water,
she watched the red carp emphasise her mouth,
saw underneath
the long green weeds lace in
through a transparency of face and skin,
smiled at herself smiling reflectively,
lending a new complexion to the sky.

In service to her beauty
long mornings lengthened to a duty
patiently served before the triple mirror
whose six eyes sent her many a time in terror
to hide in rows of whispering dresses;
but her glass soul her own three goddesses
pursued, and if she turned away,
the same three mouths would breathe "Obey, obey!"

And in procession, young men princely came,
ambassadors to her cool perfect kingdom.
Set at a distance by their praise,
she watched their unspeaking eyes adore her face.
Inside, her still self waited. Nothing moved.
Finally, by three husbands richly loved

(none of them young), she drifted into death,
the glass clouding with her last moist breath.

Changed into legend, she was given rest;
and, left alone at last,
the small mim servant shuttered in her being
peeped mousily out; and seeing
the imperious mirrors glazed and still,
whimpered forlornly down the dark hall
"Oh, grieve for my body, who would not let me be.
She, not I, was a most beautiful lady."

Small Sad Song

I am a lady
three feet small.
My voice is thin
but listen, listen.
Before I die
my modest death,
tell me what gentlemen
do with great ladies,
for thigh-high now
are the thoughts I think.

Once as a girl
I knew how to smile.
My world stayed small
as my playmates mountained.
My mother mocked me.
Dogs plagued me.
Now I am doomed
to dwell among elephants.
Sometimes I fall
in love with a bird.

I move amongst
donkeys and monkeys.
Dwarfs paw me
with stubby hands.
I cannot look at them.
There are no friends
of a suitable size.
Giants tease me.
Men do not choose me.
A hunchback loves me.

If someone moved me,
I might make
monstrous poems,
vast as my dreams;
but what can come
from a thumbnail lady?
Words like watch-ticks,
whispers, twitterings,
suitable tinkles,
nothing at all.

A Day for the Book

It was a day from a book,
steeped in its own warm juice,
heavy with smells of growing,
a day the early summer
sent to confirm its coming,
laburnum and hornbeam
bartering yellow and green.

I took
the chance that you that day were ready to take
the chance. The chance was taken,
that eye-taut silence broken.

I remember the sun on your skin
till it seemed light-thin.
I remember going in, in
to the waters of your eyes,
reflecting the sky-blue look
of the lake, with a swallow or two
cutting the air in arcs.
What was said could never be true,
told as it was in time,
but the day was true.

It is a day in a book
now, as I turn it over,
not thinking to tie it in
to any before or after.
I remember, the fire lit,
you saying something like that
and the smoke fuming out
just as you spoke.

These words are something like smoke.

Me to You

I

Summer's gone brown and, with it,
our wanderings in the shires, our ways.
Look at us now.
A shuttered house drips in Moroccan rain.
A mill sits ghostly in the green of France.

Beaches are empty now of all but pebbles.
But still, at crossroads, in senorial gardens,
we meet, sleep, wrangle, part, meet, part,
making a lodging of the heart.

Now that the sea begins to dull with winter,
and I so far, and you so far
(and home further than either),
write me a long letter,
as if from home.
          Tell me about the snowfalls
at night, and tell me how we'd sit in firelight,
hearing dogs huff in sleep, hearing the geese
hiss in the barn, hearing the horse clop home.
Say how the waterfall sounds, and how the weeds
trail in the slithering river.
Write me about the weather.

Perhaps
a letter across water,
something like this, but better,
would almost move us strangely
closer to home.

Write, and I'll come.

II

All day I have been writing you a letter.

Now, after hours of gazing at the page
and watching the screen of rain, I have enacted
a flow of endless letters in my head
(all of them different) and not one
in any written shape to send.
Those letters never end.

In between pages of wishing, I walked to the river
and wrote you of how the water
wrinkles and eddies and wanders away.
That was easier to say.

I wrote of how the snow
had fallen and turned blue,
and how the bush you wanted
could not be planted.

Some pages were all remembering—the places,
faces, frontiers, rooms, and days we went through
ages ago.
(Do you do this too?)
Always coming back to snow.

Mostly an endless, useless run of questions.
How are you now? How is it there?
Who will you and I
be in a year?
Who are we now?

Oh no,
there is no letter to send you, only this stream
of disconnected brooding, this rhythm
of wanting, cumbersome
in words, lame.

Come.

Calenture

He never lives to tell,
but other men bring back the tale

of how, after days of gazing at the sea
unfolding itself incessantly and greenly—
hillsides of water crested with clouds of foam—
he, heavy with a fading dream of home,
clambers aloft one morning and, looking down,
cries out at seeing a different green—
farms, woods, grasslands, an extending plain,
hazy meadows, a long tree-fledged horizon,
his ship riding deep in rippled grain,
swallows flashing in the halcyon sun,
the road well-known to him, the house, the garden,
figures at the gate—and, foundering in his passion,
he suddenly climbs down and begins to run.
Dazed by his joy, the others watch him drown.

Such calenture, they say,
is not unknown in lovers long at sea

yet such a like fever did she make in me
this green-leaved summer morning, that I,
seeing her confirm a wish made lovingly,
felt gate, trees, grass, birds, garden glimmer over,
a ripple cross her face, the sky quiver,
the cropped lawn away in waves, the house founder,
the light break into flecks, the path shimmer
till, finding her eyes clear and true at the centre,
I walked toward her on the flowering water.

The Figures on the Frieze

Darkness wears off and, dawning into light,
they find themselves unmagically together.
He sees the stains of morning in her face.
She shivers, distant in his bitter weather.

Diminishing of legend sets him brooding.
Great goddess-figures conjured from his book
blur what he sees with bafflement of wishing.
Sulky, she feels his fierce, accusing look.

Familiar as her own, his body's landscape
seems harsh and dull to her habitual eyes.
Mystery leaves, and, mercilessly flying,
the blind fiends come, emboldened by her cries.

Avoiding simple reach of hand for hand
(which would surrender pride) by noon they stand
withdrawn from touch, reproachfully alone,
small in each other's eyes, tall in their own.

Wild with their misery, they entangle now
in baffling agonies of why and how.
Afternoon glimmers, and they wound anew,
flesh, nerve, bone, gristle in each other's view.

''What have you done to me?'' From each proud heart,
new phantoms walk in the deceiving air.
As the light fails, each is consumed apart,
he by his ogre vision, she by her fire.

When night falls, out of a despair of daylight,
they strike the lying attitudes of love,
and through the perturbations of their bodies,
each feels the amazing, murderous legends move.

Quarrels

I can feel a quarrel blowing up in your body,
as old salts can smell storms
which are still fretting under the horizon,
before your eyes have flashed their first alarms.

Whatever the reason, the reason is not the reason.
It's a weather. It's a wellhead about to blaze gas,
flaring up when you suddenly stumble over
an alien presence in your private space.

You face me, eyes slitted like a cat's.
I can feel your nails uncurling.
The tendons in your neck twang with anger.
Your face is liquid as it is in loving.

Marking how often you say "always" and "never",
I on my side grow icy, tall, and thin
until, with watching you, I forget to listen,
and am burned through and through with your high passion.

Face to face, like wrestlers or lovers,
we spit it out. Your words nip, like bites.
Your argument's a small, tenacious creature
I try to stomp on with great logical boots.

Dear angry one, let the boots and the skittering beast
chase wildly round the room like Tom and Jerry
or who and why. Let us withdraw and watch them,
but side by side, not nose to nose and wary.

That is the only way we'll disentangle
the quarrel from ourselves and switch it off.
Not face to face. The sparks of confrontation
too easily ignite a rage like love.

The he-with-her subsides, the I-with-you
looms into place. So we fold up the words
and, with a movement much like waking up,
we turn the weather down, and turn towards.

Mandala: Dilemma

THE PEN IS MIGHTIER THAN

III

Scotland

It was a day peculiar to this piece of the planet,
when larks rose on long thin strings of singing
and the air shifted with the shimmer of actual angels.
Greenness entered the body. The grasses
shivered with presences, and sunlight
stayed like a halo on hair and heather and hills.
Walking into town, I saw, in a radiant raincoat,
the woman from the fish-shop. ''What a day it is!''
cried I, like a sunstruck madman.
And what did she have to say for it?
Her brow grew bleak, her ancestors raged in their graves
as she spoke with their ancient misery:
''We'll pay for it, we'll pay for it, we'll pay for it!''

Mediterranean

However gracefully
the spare leaves of the fig tree
abundant overhead
with native courtesy
include us in their shade,
among the rented flowers
we keep a tenant's station.
The garden is not ours.

Under the arching trellis
the gardener moves below.
Observe him on his knees
with offering of water
for roots that are not his
tendering to a power
whose name he does not know,
but whom he must appease.

So do we too accord
the windings of the vine
and swelling of the olive
a serious mute oblation
and a respectful word,
aware of having put,
in spite of cultivation,
the worm within the fruit.

This garden tenancy
tests our habitual eye.
Now, water and the moon
join what we do not own.
The rent is paid in breath,
and so we freely give
the apple tree beneath
our unpossessive love.

Dear one, this present Eden
lays down its own condition :
we should not ask to wait.
No angel drives us out,
but time, without a word,
will show among the flowers,
sure as a flaming sword.
The garden is not ours.

Galilea

Bleached white, bedazzled
by the bright light falling,
the hilltop holds me up.
Below, the coastline bares its teeth.

Winded, burned to the bone, between
the stony green of the olive,
the gray grimace of stone,
I look dazedly down.

How to come to rest
in this raw, whittled landscape
where earth, air, fire, and water
bluntly demand obeisance?

Perhaps to fix one place
in a shifting world where time
talks and where too many selves
criss-cross and demand
enactment and re-enactment,

somewhere decent to die in,
somewhere which could become
landscape and vocabulary,
equilibrium, home.

New York Surprised

I come down suddenly, out of the sky,
into this city, which I knew
well enough once to move about in by instinct.

Not now. Not now.

From the taxi window, I worry the signs, wondering
whether or not the driver knows his way
to the house I hope to be in, to the ones
whose letters said ''Come'' when I read them
on a stone beach in the garden,
twelve droning Spanish hours away.
Of course he knows his way,
but nevertheless I worry.

''There are too many people in the world''
the old postman would mumble, as he thumbed
my letters out, smelling of sweat and donkeys.

There are too many people, I say to myself anxiously.
There were too many people before, in the afternoons here
when the spring was sweet like this one, when the sun
splattered on unexpected pinks and windows
flaming, when I knew
where everyone was, when the houses
stood still in their places,
when I knew how long to wait for the door to click,
when to go home, when to be alone,
when to say ''Yes'' and be sure.

Newly arrived from nowhere,
where the only movement has been
in leaves, in water running, in the slow
flow of the day, with odd words jotted down

to hold a moment, to tell time in a letter,
I watch the towers close in and the city
awe me with windows. I nibble my nails
away with unknowing. Who will be there?
Which me will I meet from the past in the towering city
I once knew as I know
now the ways of almonds and mimosa
in the village in which I never
arrive but always am?

Only my name is the same.

Isle of Arran

Where no one was was where my world was stilled
into hills that hung behind the lasting water,
a quiet quilt of heather where bees slept,
and a single slow bird in circles winding
round the axis of my head.

Any wind being only my breath, the weather
stopped, and a woollen cloud smothered the sun.
Rust and a mist hung over the clock of the day.
A mountain dreamed in the light of the dark
and marsh mallows were yellow for ever.

Still as a fish in the secret loch alone
I was held in the water where my feet found ground
and the air where my head ended,
all thought a prisoner of the still sense—
till a butterfly drunkenly began the world.

Isla Negra, Chile

Sitting with the Pacific between my toes
in Chile, which I only knew by name,
in Isla Negra, which is not an island,
I listen across amazement to a girl
punctuating the air on a guitar.

There are places too well known to notice
and places unimaginable like dreams.
I am
suspended between the two. I know the sun
of old. I know the sea, over and over,
and once again. I do not know the girl
except by touch. The moment has no name.
After three playings, I will know the tune.

Tiree

Over the walking foreshore cluttered
black with the tide's untidy wrack,
and pools that brimmed with the moon,
I trespassed underwater.
My feet found seabed sand.
The night wore guilt like a watermark
and down the guilty dark,
the gulls muttered to windward.
Far out, the tide spoke back.

Across the morning clean of my walking
ghost and the driftwood litter,
singly I walked into singing light.

The rocks walked light on the water,
and clouds as clean as spinnakers
puffed in the sea-blue sky.
A starfish signed the sand. Beyond,
I faced the innocent sea.

Chelsea Reach

The boat rides watertight, moored, fog-shrouded.
The boy reads, floats, daydreams.
With less daylight, I get to know darkness.

Rueful winter, laying gloom on the river.
Unkind winter, contradictor of comfort.
Blank winter, an unmarked blackboard.

Evenings aboard are longer, with more remembering.
Conclusions break, a long slow march of thought.
I sit in the lamp's pool, my head in darkness.

The boy mutters lost words, the phrases of dreams.
The tide laps him to sleep, nudges him with morning.
He rises, born and beginning. To watch him is wonder.

That might be enough, the hollow hull-shelter
shrouded in winter, shipshape on the river,
the boy bright with questions, I fathering answer

but for the gathering gloom, the looming winter,
the present light breaking, change making fear,
tide on gray tide, another, another, another.

Geneva

In this town, in the blurred and snowy dawn,
under humped eaves, in a lopsided house
built, it would seem, by gnomes, in the first
hushed snowlight, in the snowy hush,
an alarm clock catches and trills time on its tongue
like a clockwork rooster. Silence. And then another
begins to burr in the attic, its small bell
nibbling at the edges of awareness.
So the day speaks. Sleep is left like fallen snow
on the tumbled snow-white bed in which we wake.

    And then the bells begin their wrangling preamble
to the hour, giving tongue, tumbling
one over the other, faltering, failing, falling
like snow on the white pillow. Their gold tongues wag
with time. (They are rung, it would seem, by gnomes).
Now, in the town, the day is on its way.

    Snowfalls nibble at the windows. In the great
assembly halls, bells ring
along the marble lobbies, calling the delegates in
to the long tables of words where, crouched
like watchmakers, they worry away
the agendas of the world, their tongues ticking
like mechanisms, and in the earphones
the voices of interpreters trill their small alarms.

    Time, gentlemen. Time is what they are telling.
The snow melts silently, the watchsprings twitter.
What was the question? Bells
telling time obscure the answer.
(The clocks never need translation.)
Eyes on the snow, we listen.
The words roll on like bells
marking time; they fall and drift like snow,
leaving their meaning in a watery
residue. The diplomats pace the halls,

watching the clock, attentive to alarms.
        All these words telling time fall thick as snowflakes.
We hope for a conclusion from the clock,
which never comes, except in intervals
of snowy silence. Clocks obscure our time.
        Now, in the town, something is ticking away.
(Gnomes can be glimpsed at night, in pools of lamplight,
peering through glass at something small and precious,
ticking, and probably gold.)
In this town of telling, we grow old
in a tumble of bells, and over us all
in the continuum   *
time falls, snow falls, words fall.

New Hampshire

Here, green has grown to be a habit.
The hills are forest-headed, not for farmers.
Trees hug the land as close as fur.
A lake looks naked. There is no way in,

except for local animals. And the roads
stumble and lurch down humps of stubbled dust.
Flowers bloom at ease without being told
and grass has grown untidily, in a hurry.

Here, the tall elm and the leaking maple,
and apple trees as gnarled as farmers' knuckles
ooze stickily with sap or syrup.
Forests are tumbled to make room for trees.

Houses are hewn and hidden in the hedges,
all pine and wooden pegs. The paths are lost.
Towns are a pilgrimage away.
Here, families live alone in hand-made homes.

Only the animals are seasoned owners.
The lakes belong to frogs with broken voices.
Farms are inhabited by rabbits.
A fox barks like a landlord down the dark.

Deer have been known to tiptoe down for apples.
A snake may suddenly scribble out of sight.
Your eyes are never sure. Each evening
someone comes back from almost seeing a bear.

Here, space is sweet with extra air. The silence
is positive, and has a steady sound.
You seem to own the woods, until
a shotgun coughs, to warn you, in the valley.

A week is a whole anthology of weather.
The country has you somehow at its mercy.
The size of the moon begins to matter,
and every night a whippoorwill leaves omens.

All names are hung on stilted mailboxes,
spasmodically fed with last week's letters.
The children quickly learn to wave.
A summer changes strangers into neighbours.

Here, one is grateful to the tolerant landscape,
and glad to be known by men with leather faces
who welcome anything but questions.
Words, like the water, must be used with care.

Flying Time

The man in the seat in front
is bald. As he reclines
his shining pate toward me,
I look up from the map
on my knee and read into his head
the red veins that connect
St Louis with Chicago,
Phoenix with Washington.
A coastline of gray hair surrounds
his neat, skintight America,
luminous, like a mirror.
I cannot see his face
but might catch sight of my own,
might face my alien
and anxious eyes. Does he
hold an America in his head,
and is the man behind
reading the back of my head?
My hair obscures my mind.
The seat-belt sign is on.
The sky is letting us down.
What waits on the ground?
Some solid, sure America,
prepared to take us in
from the nowhere of the air,
bald, mad, lost as we are?

IV

Curiosity

may have killed the cat. More likely,
the cat was just unlucky, or else curious
to see what death was like, having no cause
to go on licking paws, or fathering
litter on litter of kittens, predictably.

Nevertheless, to be curious
is dangerous enough. To distrust
what is always said, what seems,
to ask odd questions, interfere in dreams,
smell rats, leave home, have hunches,
does not endear cats to those doggy circles
where well-smelt baskets, suitable wives, good lunches
are the order of things, and where prevails
much wagging of incurious heads and tails.

Face it. Curiosity
will not cause us to die—
only lack of it will.
Never to want to see
the other side of the hill
or that improbable country
where living is an idyll
(although a probable hell)
would kill us all.
Only the curious
have if they live a tale
worth telling at all.

Dogs say cats love too much, are irresponsible,
are dangerous, marry too many wives,
desert their children, chill all dinner tables
with tales of their nine lives.

Well, they are lucky. Let them be
nine-lived and contradictory,
curious enough to change, prepared to pay
the cat-price, which is to die
and die again and again,
each time with no less pain.
A cat-minority of one
is all that can be counted on
to tell the truth; and what cats have to tell
on each return from hell
is this: that dying is what the living do,
that dying is what the loving do,
and that dead dogs are those who never know
that dying is what, to live, each has to do.

Propinquity

is the province of cats. Living by accident,
lapping the food at hand or sleeking down
in an adjacent lap when sleep occurs to them,
never aspiring to consistency
in homes or partners, unaware of property,
cats take their chances, love by need or nearness
as long as the need lasts, as long as the nearness
is near enough. The code of cats is simply
to take what comes. And those poor souls who claim
to own a cat, who long to recognise
in bland and narrowing eyes a look like love,
are bound to suffer should they expect
cats to come purring punctually home.
Home is only where the food and the fire are,

but might be anywhere. Cats fall on their feet,
nurse their own wounds, attend to their own laundry,
and purr at appropriate times. O folly, folly,
to love a cat, and yet
we dress with love the distance that they keep,
the hair-raising way they have, and easily blame
all their abandoned litters and torn ears
on some marauding tiger, well aware
that cats themselves do not care.

Yet part of us is cat. Confess—
love turns on accident and needs
nearness; and the various selves we have
accrue from our cat-wanderings, our chance
crossings. Imagination prowls at night,
cat-like, among odd possibilities.
Only our dog-sense brings us faithfully home,
makes meaning out of accident, keeps faith,
and, cat-and-dog, the arguments go at it.
But every night, outside, cat-voices call
us out to take a chance, to leave
the safety of our baskets and to let
what happens happen. "Live, live!" they catcall.
"Each moment is your next! Propinquity,
propinquity is all!"

Cat-Faith

As a cat, caught by the door opening,
on the perilous top shelf, red-jawed and raspberry-clawed,
lets itself fall floorward without looking,
sure by cat-instinct it will find the ground,

where innocence is; and falls
anyhow, in a furball, so fast that the eye
misses the twist and trust
that come from having fallen before,
and only notices cat silking away,
crime inconceivable in so meek a walk:

so do we let ourselves fall morningward
through shelves of dream. When, libertine at dark,
we let the visions in, and the black window
grotesques us back, our world unbalances.
Many-faced monsters of our own devising
jostle on the verge of sleep, as the room
loses its edges and grows hazed and haunted
by words murmured or by woes remembered,
till, sleep-dissolved, we fall, the known world leaves us,
and room and dream and self and safety melt
into a final madness, where any landscape
may easily curdle, and the dead cry out . . .

but ultimately, it ebbs. Voices recede.
The pale square of the window glows and stays.
Slowly the room arrives and dawns, and we
arrive in our selves. Last night, last week, the past
leak back, awake. As light solidifies,
dream dims. Outside, the washed hush of the garden
waits patiently and, newcomers from death,
how gratefully we draw its breath!
Yet, to endure that unknown night by night,
must we not be sure, with cat-insight,
we can afford its terrors, and that full day
will find us at the desk, sane, unafraid—
cheeks shaven, letters written, bills paid?

Ghosts

Never to see ghosts? Then to be
haunted by what is, only, to believe that glass
is for looking through, that rooms too can be empty,
the past past, deeds done,
that sleep, however troubled, is your own.
Do the dead lie down, then? Are blind men blind?
Does love rest in the senses? Do lights go out?
And what is that shifting, shifting in the mind?
The wind?

No, they are with us. Let your ear be gentle.
At dawn or owl-cry, over doorway and lintel,
theirs are the voices moving night towards morning,
the garden's grief, the river's warning.
Their curious presence in a kiss,
the past quivering in what is,
our words odd-sounding, not our own—
how can we think we sleep alone?

What do they have to tell? If we can hear them,
their voices are denials of all dying,
faint, like a lost bell-tone, lying
beyond sound or belief, in the oblique
reach of the sense through layers of recognition . . . .
Ghost by my desk, speak, speak.

Pigeons

On the crooked arm of Columbus, on his cloak,
they mimic his blind and statuary stare,
and the chipped profiles of his handmaidens
they adorn with droppings. Over the loud square,
from all the arms and ledges of their rest,
only a breadcrust or a bell unshelves them.
Adding to Atlas' globe, they dispose themselves
with a fat propriety, and pose as garlands
importantly about his burdened shoulders.
Occasionally a lift of wind uncarves them.

Stone becomes them; they in their turn become it.
Their opal eyes have a monumental cast.
And, in a maze of noise,
their quiet *croomb croomb* dignifies the spaces,
suggesting the sound of silence. On cobbled islands,
marooned in tantrums of traffic, they know their place.
Faithful and anonymous, like servants,
they never beg, but properly receive.

Arriving in rainbows of oil-and-water feathers,
they fountain down from buttresses and outcrops,
from Fontainebleau and London,
and, perched on the margins of roofs, with a gargoyle look,
they note, from an edge of air, with hooded eyes,
the city slowly lessening the sky.

All praise to them who nightly in the parks
keep peace for us; who, cosmopolitan,
patrol and people all cathedralled places,
the paved courts of the past, pompous as keepers,
and easily, lazily haunt and inhabit

St Paul's, St Peter's, or the Madeleine—
a sober race of messengers and custodians,
neat in their international uniforms,
alighting with a word perhaps from Rome.
Permanence is their business, space and time
their special preservations; and wherever
the great stone men we save from death are stationed,
appropriately on the head of each is perched,
as though for ever, his appointed pigeon.

Foreigners

Owls, like monks of a rare, feathered order,
haunt one aloof, lopped tower in this
unlikely city, cresting the broken stones
like ghosts at dusk, watchful, wary,
describing soft, slow curves in the falling sky.

Supremely odd and patiently oblivious
to all but wind and owlhood, they tatter
the evening air with their broad, sooty wings.
And over all, the tower seems content
with its alien colony. For whose is a city?

Yet below, the jabbering birds of the sprawled suburbs
complain from the lower roofs, look up from crusts
and blame owls for the dust, for all the dismal
workaday winging. The atmosphere is crowded,
to their native eyes, with a woeful weight of owls.

What do the owls answer? To wit, nothing.
And sure enough, with time passing, the tower
becomes a landmark mentioned in the guidebooks
with owls as appropriate appendages. The city
absorbs them into its anonymous air.

Now other birds alight on the battlements,
occasionally singing. Not worthwhile to war
over a lack of crumbs, in alien weather.
Who gives a hoot, say owls. The wind is common.
Let all poor birds be brothers under the feather.

Daedalus

My son has birds in his head.

I know them now. I catch
the pitch of their calls, their shrill
cacophonies, their chitterings, their coos.
They hover behind his eyes and come to rest
on a branch, on a book, grow still,
claws curled, wings furled.
His is a bird world.

I learn the flutter of his moods,
his moments of swoop and soar.
From the ground I feel him try
the limits of the air—
sudden lift, sudden terror—
and move in time to cradle
his quivering, feathered fear.

At evening, in the tower,
I see him to sleep and see
the hooding-over of eyes,
the slow folding of wings.
I wake to his morning twitterings,
to the *croomb* of his becoming.

He chooses his selves—wren, hawk,
swallow or owl—to explore
the trees and rooftops of his heady wishing.
Tomtit, birdwit.
Am I to call him down, to give him
a grounding, teach him gravity?
Gently, gently.
Time tells us what we weigh, and soon enough
his feet will reach the ground.
Age, like a cage, will enclose him.
So the wise men said.

My son has birds in his head.

Frog Dream

Nightlong, frogs in the pool
croak out calamity till, wakeful,
I interpret each crooked syllable.

The sound is churlish, coarse—
frog words grating out a hoarse
chorus of drowned remorse,

as I do, in half-sleep,
until, drifting, I cannot keep
the dark from deepening

or dream voices from becoming
peepers and grunters, churning
my madness over. The pool is lapping,

weed-streaked, in my head.
Frogs echo from the edges of the bed,
in the grieving voices of the long dead,

grudges long hidden in their old throats,
hauntings, water horror, hates.
My fear is a slow crescendo of frog notes . . . .

Later, awake in the sanity of dawn,
I walk to the pool, limpid under the sun.
What did I dream? The frogs have all gone down.

The Colour of Herring

I read in the fishbooks that the herring
is black-backed and silver-sided,
is blue-flecked and silver-faceted,
is gray-green shot with silver,
is black and green and silver,
is blue and glass.
I find the herring in my hands
has all the silver of the evening,
all the blue of the bay,
all the green of the deep sea over the side.
The black may easily be in my mood.
The silver certainly flakes my sleeve.

But over my hands in its dying moment spills
the herring's blood
which, silver, green, black, blue aside,
runs unmistakably red.

What's What

Most people know
the story of how
the frog was a prince
and the dragon was ticklish,
or how the princess
grew fat in the end;
nevertheless,
think of the chance
the youngest son took—
gloom to the left of him,
groans to the right of him,
no spell to tell him
which way to take,
no map, no book,
no real interest.
All he could say was
"Maybe I'm me"
but he knew not to trust
the wizards who seemed,
the bird with the breast
of too many colours,
the princess who hummed
too perfect a song.

The going was not good
but his curious head
said over and over
ridiculous words
like *quince* and *fray bentos*
all through the wood.
"Yes," he said firmly,
"nobody pays me,
nobody knows me,
so I will decide
which tree will amaze me
when I see a leaf
I can be sure of.
Whom do I listen to?
Not that toad
with the gem in its head,
nor that mole that mumbles
precise directions,
nor the nice wizard,
so soft and helpful,
nor mild old women
gathering wood.
It's that clumsy bird
who looks askance
with only one eye—
untidy feathers,
flying absent-mindedly,
out in all weathers,
little to say—
he's for me.
He's not after
a cut of the treasure.
He knows well
that he's going nowhere
and, what's more,
he doesn't care.

If I'd listened to witches
and looked in crystals,
I'd be expert
at going wrong,
but I know my birdsong.
Hearing his *tip-tippy*,
I know who *he* is.
I'll go *his* way.

Needless to say,
the youngest son won
with enough to go on;
and the one-eyed bird,
whoever he was,
went *tip-tip-tippy*
to pleasure his own
well-worn feathers,
over and over,
with no one to hear . . .

Then, one day,
the youngest son
had a youngest son,
and so on.

V

Weathering

I am old enough now for a tree
once planted, knee high, to have grown to be
twenty times me,

and to have seen babies marry, and heroes grow deaf—
but that's enough meaning-of-life.
It's living through time we ought to be connoisseurs of.

From wearing a face all this time, I am made aware
of the maps faces are, of the inside wear and tear.
I take to faces that have come far.

In my father's carved face, the bright eye
he sometimes would look out of, seeing a long way
through all the tree-rings of his history.

I am awed by how things weather: an oak mantel
in the house in Spain, fingered to a sheen,
the marks of hands leaned into the lintel,

the tokens in the drawer I sometimes touch—
a crystal lived-in on a trip, the watch
my father's wrist wore to a thin gold sandwich.

It is an equilibrium
which breasts the cresting seasons but still stays calm
and keeps warm. It deserves a good name.

Weathering. Patina, gloss, and whorl.
The trunk of the almond tree, gnarled but still fruitful.
Weathering is what I would like to do well.

Outlook, Uncertain

No season
brings conclusion.

Each year,
through heartache, nightmare,

true loves alter,
marriages falter,

and lovers illumine
the antique design,

apart, together,
foolish as weather,

right as rain,
sure as ruin.

Must you, then, and I
adjust the whole sky

over every morning?
Or else, submitting

to cloud and storm,
enact the same

lugubrious ending,
new lives pending?

James Bottle's Year

December finds him
outside, looking skyward.
The year gets a swearword.

His rage is never permanent.
By January he's out,
silent and plough-bent.

All white February,
he's in a fury
of wind-grief and ground-worry.

By March, he's back
scouring the ground for luck,
for rabbit-run and deer-track.

April is all sounds and smiles.
The hill is soft with animals.
His arms describe miles.

The local girls say
he's honeyed and bee-headed
at haytime in May.

In June,
he'll stay up late, he'll moon
and talk to children.

No one sees him in July.
At dawn, he'll ride away
with distance in his eye.

In August, you'd assume
yourself to be almost welcome.
He keeps open time.

But, on one September morning,
you'll see cloud-worries form.
His eyes flash storm warnings.

October is difficult.
He tries to puzzle out
If it's his or the season's fault.

In November, he keeps still
through hail and snowfall,
thinking through it all.

What's causing the odd weather?
Himself, or the capricious air?
Or the two together?

December, breathing hard,
he's back outside, hurling skyward
his same swearword.

1973

Lean, mean year, breeder of obituaries.
Funereal year, you earned a black border.
Half-masted year, we thankfully cover you over.

You claimed the long-lived ones, Casals, Picasso;
Neruda and Chile both, in one rank breath.
You gorged yourself on armies, tribes, and children.

Robbing the present to enrich the past,
you leave us as a string of cruel ciphers.
Your notes and dates are permanent in stone.

Corrosive months, counting us down in deathbells.
Gray ghoulish months of crows and cruel weather.
Meat-eating months, you trained us in despair.

Although we spite you now by seeing you out,
be confident that you will be remembered,
bitch year, burier, bearer of famous dark.

That Dying: November 23, 1963

As often as not, on fair days, there is time
for words to flex their muscles, to strut like peacocks,
discovering what to say in the act of saying—
the music of meaning emerging from the sound
of the words playing.

Every now and again, however, the glass breaks,
the alarm shrills, the women hide their faces.
It is then that words jump to their feet and rush,
like white-faced stretcher-bearers,
tight-lipped, tense, to the unspeakable scene.
They grab air, water, syllables, anything handy.
There is blood. No nonsense. No adjectives. No time.

O that words could have been
a tourniquet of a kind, to keep
that exuberant life from spattering away,
instead of, as now, a dirge, a bell
tolling, a stutter, a sigh, silence.

There is nothing now for these words to do
but walk away aimlessly, mute, like mourners.

Stalemate

Shrill interruption
of children's voices
raised in the garden.
Two of them stand
face to face,
each in one hand
weighing a stone,
each on his own
rigid ground.

You drop your stone,
then I'll drop mine.
No, you first.
Put yours down.
But if I do,
you'll throw yours.
Promise I won't.
I don't believe you.
Cross your heart?
Cross my heart.

Easy to call
the children in
before blows fall,
but not to settle
the ruffled feel
the garden has
as they both echo
the endless bicker
of lovers and statesmen,
learnt so soon.

Who began it?
Now, no matter.
The air is taut
with accusation.
Despair falls
like a cold stone
crossing the heart.
How did it start?
A children's quarrel.
What is its end?
The death of love.
The doom of all.

Black Holes

It happens on a walk. Quite suddenly
a black hole of horror opens in the road

as I recall a cruelty I did
and gasp as the hole engulfs me, the horror chokes me.

I cry out at the memory. The shame
grows hot enough to sear me.

I keep a collection of those painful moments.
Shame's a proper servant of clarity.

Sweating, I usher a surprised old woman
across the road, avoiding the black hole.

L'Amour de Moi

The tune at first is odd, though still familiar.
It asks and answers, as you hear
the children playing it on their thin recorders
over and over in the afternoon,
through breath and error, with the huge blue day
hovering overhead. The house dozes,
and guests asleep—uncles, grandmothers, cousins—
accept it easily into their dreams,
like variations on the same cool breeze,
and sigh. The notes, frail moths among the roses,
falter but never fail. A wind passes,
and then the tune again, the first phrase firm,
the second wavering and fanciful,
the last settling, as the air falls still.

Later, at night, its counterpoint—
the family after dinner, lifting down
instruments from the walls, and their huge shadows
huddled, bending together, as candle flames
waver with the first enquiring chord.
Sisters, sweethearts, friends, they yield to the air,
subscribed by lifting strings and the bland oboe,
gloom of the cello, thump of drum.
The children turn in sleep upstairs, dreaming
in waves that widen from their own small music—
heartbeat and breath, the fanciful lift of fiddles,
the falling arm, the last cool phrase, falling.
Shadows pause in their place. Outside,
the garden breathes beneath suspended stars.

This is true harmony, and in this tune
turn families, passions, histories, planets, all.

The Fall

He teeters along the crumbling top
of the garden wall and calls, "Look up,
Papa, look up! I'm flying . . . " till,
in a sudden foreseen spasm, I see him fall.

Terrible
when fear cries to the senses, when the whirl
of the possible drowns the real. Falling
is a fright in me. I call
and move in time to catch
his small, sweat-beaded body,
still thrilled with the air.
"I flew, Papa, I flew!"
"I know, child, I know."

The Spiral

The seasons of this year are in my luggage.
Now, lifting the last picture from the wall,
I close the eyes of the room. Each footfall
clatters on the bareness of the stair.
The family ghosts fade in the hanging air.
Mirrors reflect the silence. There is no message.
I wait in the still hall for a car to come.
Behind, the house will dwindle to a name.

Places, addresses, faces left behind.
The present is a devious wind
obliterating days and promises.
Tomorrow is a tinker's guess.
Marooned in cities, dreaming of greenness,
or dazed by journeys, dreading to arrive—
change, change is where I live.

For possibility,
I choose to leave behind
each language, each country.
Will this place be an end,
or will there be one other,
truer, rarer?

Often now, in dream,
abandoned landscapes come,
figuring a constant theme:
Have you left us behind?
What have you still to find?

Across the spiral distance,
through time and turbulence,
the rooted self in me
maps out its true country.

And, as my father found
his own small weathered island,
so will I come to ground

where that small man, my son,
can put his years on.

For him, too, time will turn.

VI

An Instance

Perhaps the accident of a bird
crossing the green window, a simultaneous phrase
of far singing, and a steeplejack
poised on the church spire, changing the gold clock,
set the moment alight. At any rate, a word
in that instant of realising catches fire,
ignites another, and soon the page is ablaze
with a wildfire of writing. The clock chimes in the square.

All afternoon, in a scrawl of time,
the mood still smoulders. Rhyme remembers rhyme,
and words summon the moment when amazement
ran through the senses like a flame.
Later, the song forgotten, the sudden bird
flown who-knows-where, the incendiary word
long since crossed out, the steeplejack gone home,
their moment burns again, restored
to its spontaneity. The poem stays.

Querida Mañana

Mañana—and an accompanying
cosmic shrug to say :
May this small incantation
keep what is still to happen
suitably far away.

In this rock-cluttered valley,
where sheep-bells tinkle time
irregularly on the ear,
and where a call will carry
across to the opposite hill,
all hangs in a continuum,
and what will happen, what befall,
seems more a matter of accident
than ever of will.

Mañana. Dear tomorrow.
The unknown in a nutshell,
invoked to give us breath,
to slough decision off,
to keep the world of Yes and No
at least a day away.

So, when the children
come trailing hopefully in
with question-marks for eyes,
looking for a word
to hang their wishing on,
mañana reassures them.
They echo it like a spell.
Tomorrow, at a distance,
will certainly be well.

The Syntax of Seasons

Autumn was adjectival. I recall
a gray, dank, gnarled spell
when all wore fall-quality, a bare
mutating atmosphere.

Winter hardened into nouns. Withdrawn
in lamplight, I would crown
the cold with thought-exactitude, would claim
the drear air with a name.

In spring, all language loosened and became
less in demand, limping, lame,
before the bursting days. What told
was tongue-tied wonder at the green and gold.

Steeped now in summer, though our chattering
rises and falls, occasional as birdsong,
we fall to silence under the burning sun,
and feel the great verbs run.

Visiting Lecturer

As travelling becomes arriving,
I land, with language in my luggage,
a change of tense, to make sense of a place,
to make myself intelligible. A page
of plans turns into people, faces, voices;

and, once unpacked, my words explore
the oddness of the air,
the face the place wears and the weather
settling into saying. All the names
provide a new vocabulary, to answer
who I am, what is what, where we are.

In the lull between seeing and saying,
I wonder at the way words have
of hardening and betraying:
but sense and sound assert themselves
beyond conclusion and become
a temporary, articulated home,
a resting-place
aloof from time and space.

But only for a time. Time tells
itself through spells and sudden oracles,
and afterwards I gather
folding vocabularies
and stuff an itinerant syntax
into a silent file.
Even though words are portable,
where can they come to rest?

At best,
time dwindles down, and words
prepare to be goodbyes, and then take up
their stations in the book.
The place remains in a diary and the mind,
moving, continues undefined.

Home
is where new words are still to come.

The Academy

I do not think of the academy
in the whirl of days. It does not change. I do.
The place hangs in my past like an engraving.
I went back once to lay a wreath on it,
and met discarded selves I scarcely knew.

It has a lingering aura, leather bindings,
a smell of varnish and formaldehyde,
a certain dusty holiness in the cloisters.
We used to race our horses on the sand
away from it, manes flying, breathing hard.

Trailing to the library of an afternoon,
we saw the ivy crawling underneath
the labyrinthine bars on the window ledges.
I remember the thin librarian's look of hate
as we left book holes in her shelves, like missing teeth.

On evenings doomed by bells, we felt the sea
creep up, we heard the temperamental gulls
wheeling in clouds about the kneeworn chapel.
They keened on the knifing wind like student souls.
Yet we would dent the stones with our own footfalls.

Students still populate the place, bright starlings,
their notebooks filled with scribbled parrot-answers
to questions they unravel every evening
in lamplit pools of spreading argument.
They slash the air with theory, like fencers.

Where is the small, damp-browed professor now?
Students have pushed him out to sea in a boat
of lecture-notes. Look, he bursts into flame!
How glorious a going for one whose words
had never struck a spark on the whale-road.

And you will find retainers at their posts,
wearing their suits of age, brass buttons, flannel,
patrolling lawns they crop with careful scissors.
They still will be in silver-haired attendance
to draw lines through our entries in the annals.

It is illusion, the academy.
In truth, the ideal talking-place to die.
Only the landscape keeps a sense of growing.
The towers are floating on a shifting sea.
You did not tell the truth there, nor did I.

Think of the process—moments becoming poems
which stiffen into books in the library,
and later, lectures, books about the books,
footnotes and dates, a stone obituary.
Do you wonder that I shun the academy?

It anticipates my dying, turns to stone
too quickly for my taste. It is a language
nobody speaks, refined to ritual:
the precise writing on the blackboard wall,
the drone of requiem in the lecture hall.

I do not think much of the academy
in the drift of days. It does not change. I do.
This poem will occupy the library
but I will not. I have not done with doing.
I did not know the truth there, nor did you.

The O-Filler

One noon in the library, I watched a man—
imagine!—filling in O's, a little, rumpled
nobody of a man, who licked his stub of pencil
and leaned over every O with a loving care,
shading it neatly, exactly to its edges
until the open pages
were pocked and dotted with solid O's, like towns
and capitals on a map. And yet, so peppered,
the book appeared inhabited and complete.

That whole afternoon, as the light outside softened
and the library groaned woodenly,
he worked and worked, his o-so-patient shading
descending like an eyelid over each open O
for page after page. Not once did he miss one,
or hover even a moment over an *a*
or an *e* or a *p* or a *g*. Only the O's—
oodles of O's, O's multitudinous, O's manifold,
O's italic and roman.
And what light on his crumpled face when he discovered—
as I supposed—odd words like *zoo* and *ooze*,
polo, *oolong* and *odontology*!

Think now. In that limitless library,
all round the steep-shelved walls, bulging in their bindings,
books stood, waiting. Heaven knows how many
he had so far filled, but still there remained
uncountable volumes of O-laden prose, and odes
with inflated capital O's (in the manner of Shelley),
O-bearing Bibles and biographies,
even whole sections devoted to O alone,
all his for the filling. Glory, glory, glory!

How utterly open and endless the world must have seemed to him,
how round and ample! Think of it. A pencil
was all he needed. Life was one wide O.

And why, at the end of things, should O's not be closed
as eyes are? I envied him, for in my place
across the table from him, had I accomplished
anything as firm as he had, or as fruitful?
What could I show? A handful of scrawled lines,
an afternoon yawned and wondered away,
and a growing realisation that in time
even my scribbled words would come
under his grubby thumb, and the blinds be drawn
on all my O's, with only this thought for comfort—
that when he comes to this poem, a proper joy
may amaze his wizened face and, o, a pure pleasure
make his meticulous pencil quiver.

A Lesson in Music

Play the tune again: but this time
with more regard for the movement at the source of it
and less attention to time. Time falls
curiously in the course of it.

Play the tune again: not watching
your fingering, but forgetting, letting flow
the sound till it surrounds you. Do not count
or even think. Let go.

Play the tune again: but try to be
nobody, nothing, as though the pace
of the sound were your heart beating, as though
the music were your face.

Play the tune again. It should be easier
to think less every time of the notes, of the measure.
It is all an arrangement of silence. Be silent, and then
play it for your pleasure.

Play the tune again; and this time, when it ends,
do not ask me what I think. Feel what is happening
strangely in the room as the sound glooms over
you, me, everything.

Now,
play the tune again.

A Lesson in Handwriting

Try first this figure 2,
how, from the point of the pen,
clockwise it unwinds itself
downward to the line,
making itself a pedestal to stand on.
Watch now. Before your eyes it becomes a swan
drifting across the page, its neck so carefully
poised, its inky eye

lowered in modesty.
As you continue, soon,
between the thin blue lines,
swan after swan sails beautifully past you,
margin to margin, 2 by 2 by 2,
a handwritten swirl of swans.
Under them now unroll
the soft, curled pillows of the 6's,
the acrobatic 3's, the angular 7's,
the hourglass 8's and the neat tadpole 9's,
each passing in review
on stilts and wheels and platforms
in copybook order.

Turn the page, for now
comes the alphabet, an eccentric
parade of odd characters. Initially you may tangle
now and again in a loop or a twirl,
but patience, patience. Each in time will dawn
as faces and animals do, familiar,
laughable, crooked, quirky.
Begin with the letter S. Already
it twists away from the point like a snake or a watchspring,
coiled up and back to strike. SSSS, it says,
hissing and slithering off into the ferns of the F's.
Next comes a line of stately Q's floating
just off the ground, tethered by their tails,
over the folded arms of the W's
and the akimbo M's. Open-eyed, the O's
roll after them like bubbles or balloons
flown by the serious three-tongued E's.
See now how the page fills up
with all the furniture of writing—the armchair H's,
the ladders and trestles of A's and Y's and X's,
the T-shaped tables and the upholstered B's.
The pen abandons a whole scaffolding

of struts and braces, springs and balances,
on which will rest eventually
the weight of a written world, storey on storey
of words and signatures, all the long-drawn-out telling
that pens become repositories of.
These are now your care, and you may give them
whatever slant or human twist you wish,
if it should please you. But you will not alter
their scrawled authority, durable
as stone, silent, grave, oblivious
of all you make them tell.

Tomorrow, words begin.

Speaking a Foreign Language

How clumsy on the tongue, these acquired idioms,
after the innuendos of our own. How far
we are from foreigners, what faith
we rest in one sentence, hoping a smile will follow
on the appropriate face, always wallowing
between what we long to say and what we can,
trusting the phrase is suitable to the occasion,
the accent passable, the smile real,
always asking the traveller's fearful question—
what is being lost in translation?

Something, to be sure. And yet, to hear
the stumbling of foreign friends, how little we care
for the wreckage of word or tense. How endearing they are,
and how our speech reaches out, like a helping hand,
or limps in sympathy. Easy to understand,
through the tangle of language, the heart behind
groping toward us, to make the translation of
syntax into love.

Translator to Poet

For Pablo Neruda, 1904–1973

There are only the words left now. They lie like tombstones
or the stone Andes where the green scrub ends.
I do not have the heart to chip away
at your long lists of joy, which alternate
their iron and velvet, all the vegetation
and whalebone of your chosen stormy coast.
So much was written hope, with every line
extending life by saying, every meeting
ending in expectation of the next.
It was your slow intoning voice which counted,
bringing a living Chile into being
where poetry was bread, where books were banquets.
Now they are silent, stony on the shelf.
I cannot read them for the thunderous silence,
the grief of Chile's dying and your own,
death being the one definitive translation.

What Gets Lost/Lo Que Se Pierde

I keep translating *traduzco continuamente*
entre palabras words *que no son las mias*
into other words which are mine *de palabras a mis palabras.*
Y finalmente de quien es el texto?
Who do words belong to?
Del escritor o del traductor writer, translator
o de los idiomas or to language itself?
Traductores, somos fantasmas que viven
entre aquel mundo y el nuestro
translators are ghosts who live
in a limbo between two worlds
pero poco a poco me ocurre
que el problema no es cuestion
de lo que se pierde en traducion
the problem is not a question
of what gets lost in translation
sino but rather *lo que se pierde*
what gets lost
entre la ocurrencia—sea de amor o de agonia
between the happening of love or pain
y el hecho de que llega
a existir en palabras
and their coming into words.

Para nosotros todos, amantes, habladores
for lovers or users of words
el problema es este this is the difficulty—
lo que se pierde what gets lost
no es lo que se pierde en traducion sino
is not what gets lost in translation but more
what gets lost in language itself *lo que se pierde*
en el hecho en la lengua,
en la palabra misma.

VII

Translations

The only possible translation is poetic transmutation
or metaphor. But I would also say that in writing
an original poem we are translating the world,
transmuting it. Everything we do is translation,
and all translations are in a way creations.

Octavio Paz

H

Roman Conversation

In Rome that poet told me:
"You cannot imagine how it saddens me to see you
writing ephemeral prose in magazines."

There are weeds in the Forum. The wind
adulterates the pollen with dust.

Under the great marble sun, Rome changes
from ochre to yellow,
to sepia, to bronze.

Everywhere something is breaking down.
Our times are cracking.
It is summer
and you cannot walk through Rome.
So much grandeur enslaved. Chariots
charge against both men and cities.
Companies and phalanxes and legions,
missiles and coffins,
scrap-iron,
ruins which will be ruins.

Grasses grow,
adventitious seeds in the marble,
and garbage in the unremembering streets:
tin cans, paper, scrap.
The consumer cycle: affluence
is measured by its detritus.

It is hot. We keep on walking.
I have no wish to answer
or to question myself
if anything written today
will make a mark
any deeper than the pollen in the ruins.

Possibly our verses will last as long
as a '69 Ford
(and certainly not as long as a Volkswagen).

José Emilio Pacheco

High Treason

I do not love my country. Its abstract lustre
is beyond my grasp.
But (although it sounds bad) I would give my life
for ten places in it, for certain people,
seaports, pinewoods, fortresses,
a run-down city, gray, grotesque,
various figures from its history,
mountains
(and three or four rivers).

José Emilio Pacheco

Don't Ask Me How the Time Goes Past

Winter comes to our venerable house
and across the air pass flocks of migrating birds.
Later, spring will be born again,
the flowers you sowed will come to life.
But we,
we shall never know again
that sweet condition which was ours together.

José Emilio Pacheco

The Great Tablecloth

When they were called to the table,
the tyrants came rushing
with their temporary ladies,
it was fine to watch the women pass
like wasps with big bosoms
followed by those pale
and unfortunate public tigers.

The peasant in the field ate
his poor quota of bread,
he was alone, it was late,
he was surrounded by wheat,
but he had no more bread;
he ate it with grim teeth,
looking at it with hard eyes.

In the blue hour of eating,
the infinite hour of the roast,
the poet abandons his lyre,
takes up his knife and fork,
puts his glass on the table,
and the fishermen attend
the little sea of the soup bowl.
Burning potatoes protest
among the tongues of oil.
The lamb is gold on its coals
and the onion undresses.
It is sad to eat in dinner clothes,
like eating in a coffin,
but eating in convents
is like eating underground.
Eating alone is a disappointment,
but not eating matters more,
is hollow and green, has thorns
like a chain of fish-hooks
trailing from the heart,
clawing at your insides.

Hunger feels like pincers,
like the bite of crabs,
it burns, burns and has no fire.
Hunger is a cold fire.
Let us sit down soon to eat

with all those who haven't eaten;
let us spread great tablecloths,
put salt in the lakes of the world,
set up planetary bakeries,
tables with strawberries in snow,
and a plate like the moon itself
from which we can all eat.

For now I ask no more
than the justice of eating.

Pablo Neruda

How Much Happens in a Day

In the course of a day we shall meet one another.

But, in one day, things spring to life—
they sell grapes in the street,
tomatoes change their skin,
the young girl you wanted
never came back to the office.

They changed the postman suddenly.
The letters now are not the same.
A few golden leaves, and it's different;
this tree is now well-off.

Who would have said that the earth
with its ancient skin would change so much?
It has more volcanoes than yesterday,
the sky has brand-new clouds,
the rivers are flowing differently.
Besides, so much has come into being!

I have inaugurated hundreds
of highways and buildings,
delicate, clean bridges
like ships or violins.

And so, when I greet you
and kiss your flowering mouth,
our kisses are other kisses,
our mouths are other mouths.

Joy, my love, joy in all things,
in what falls and what flourishes.

Joy in today and yesterday,
the day before and tomorrow.

Joy in bread and stone,
joy in fire and rain.

In what changes, is born, grows,
consumes itself, and becomes a kiss again.

Joy in the air we have,
and in what we have of earth.

When our life dries up,
only the roots remain to us,
and the wind is cold like hate.

Then let us change our skin,
our nails, our blood, our gazing,
and you kiss me and I go out
to sell light on the roads.

Joy in the night and the day,
and the four stations of the soul.

Pablo Neruda

Horses

From the window I saw the horses.

I was in Berlin, in winter. The light
was without light, the sky skyless.

The air white like a moistened loaf.

From my window, I could see a deserted arena,
a circle bitten out by the teeth of winter.

All at once, led out by a single man,
ten horses were stepping, stepping into the snow.

Scarcely had they rippled into existence
like flame, than they filled the whole world of my eyes,
empty till now. Faultless, flaming,
they stepped like ten gods on broad, clean hoofs,
their manes recalling a dream of salt spray.

Their rumps were globes, were oranges.

Their colour was amber and honey, was on fire.

Their necks were towers
carved from the stone of pride,
and in their furious eyes, sheer energy
showed itself, a prisoner inside them.

And there, in the silence, at the mid-
point of the day, in a dirty, disgruntled winter,
the horses' intense presence was blood,
was rhythm, was the beckoning light of all being.

I saw, I saw, and seeing, I came to life.
There was the unwitting fountain, the dance of gold, the sky,
the fire that sprang to life in beautiful things.

I have obliterated that gloomy Berlin winter.

I shall not forget the light from these horses.

Pablo Neruda

Cat's Dream

How neatly a cat sleeps,
sleeps with its paws and its posture,
sleeps with its wicked claws,
and with its unfeeling blood,
sleeps with all the rings—
a series of burnt circles—
which have formed the odd geology
of its sand-coloured tail.

I should like to sleep like a cat,
with all the fur of time,
with a tongue rough as flint,
with the dry sex of fire;
and after speaking to no-one,
stretch myself over the world,
over roofs and landscapes,
with a passionate desire
to hunt the rats in my dreams.

I have seen how the cat asleep
would undulate, how the night
flowed through it like dark water;
and at times, it was going to fall
or possibly plunge into
the bare deserted snowdrifts.
Sometimes it grew so much in sleep
like a tiger's great-grandfather,
and would leap in the darkness over
rooftops, clouds, and volcanoes.

Sleep, sleep, cat of the night,
with episcopal ceremony
and your stone-carved moustache.
Take care of all our dreams;
control the obscurity
of our slumbering prowess
with your relentless heart
and the great ruff of your tail.

Pablo Neruda

Emerging

A man says yes without knowing
how to decide even what the question is,
and is caught up, and then is carried along
and never again escapes from his own cocoon;
and that's how we are, forever falling
into the deep well of other beings;

and one thread wraps itself around our necks,
another entwines a foot, and then it is impossible,
impossible to move except in the well—
nobody can rescue us from other people.

It seems as if we don't know how to speak;
it seems as if there are words which escape,
which are missing, which have gone away and left us
to ourselves, tangled up in snares and threads.

And all at once, that's it; we no longer know
what it's all about, but we are deep inside it,
and now we will never see with the same eyes
as once we did when we were children playing.
Now these eyes are closed to us,
now our hands emerge from different arms.

And therefore, when you sleep, you are alone in your dreaming,
and running freely through the corridors
of one dream only, which belongs to you.
Oh never let them come to steal our dreams,
never let them entwine us in our bed.
Let us hold on to the shadows
to see if, from our own obscurity,
we emerge and grope along the walls,
lie in wait for the light, to capture it,
till, once and for all time,
it becomes our own, the sun of every day.

Pablo Neruda

We Are Many

Of the many men who I am, who we are,
I can't find a single one;
they disappear among my clothes,
they've left for another city.

When everything seems to be set
to show me off as intelligent,
the fool I always keep hidden
takes over all that I say.

At other times, I'm asleep
among distinguished people,
and when I look for my brave self,
a coward unknown to me
rushes to cover my skeleton
with a thousand fine excuses.

When a decent house catches fire,
instead of the fireman I summon,
an arsonist bursts on the scene,
and that's me. What can I do?
What can I do to distinguish myself?
How can I pull myself together?

All the books I read
are full of dazzling heroes,
always sure of themselves.
I die with envy of them;
and in films full of wind and bullets,
I goggle at the cowboys,
I even admire the horses.

But when I call for a hero,
out comes my lazy old self;
so I never know who I am,
nor how many I am or will be.
I'd love to be able to touch a bell
and summon the real me,
because if I really need myself,
I mustn't disappear.

While I am writing, I'm far away;
and when I come back, I've gone.
I would like to know if others
go through the same things that I do,
have as many selves as I have,
and see themselves similarly;
and when I've exhausted this problem,
I'm going to study so hard
that when I explain myself,
I'll be talking geography.

Pablo Neruda

Consequences

He was good, the man, sure
as his hoe and his plough.
He didn't even have time
to dream while he slept.

He was poor to the point of sweat.
He was worth a single horse.

His son today is very proud
and is worth a number of cars.

He speaks with a senator's voice,
he walks with an ample step,
has forgotten his peasant father
and discovered ancestors.
He thinks like a fat newspaper,
makes money night and day,
is important even asleep.

The sons of the son are many,
they married some time ago.
They do nothing, but they consume.
They're worth thousands of mice.

The sons of the sons of the son—
what will they make of the world?
Will they turn out good or bad?
Worth flies or worth wheat?

You don't want to answer me.

But the questions do not die.

Pablo Neruda

Past

We have to discard the past
and, as one builds
floor by floor, window by window,
and the building rises,
so do we keep shedding—
first, broken tiles,
then proud doors,

until, from the past,
dust falls
as if it would crash
against the floor,
smoke rises
as if it were on fire,
and each new day
gleams
like an empty
plate.
There is nothing, there was always nothing.
It all has to be filled
with a new, expanding
fruitfulness;
then, down
falls yesterday
as in a well
falls yesterday's water,
into the cistern
of all that is now without voice, without fire.
It is difficult
to get bones used
to disappearing,
to teach eyes
to close,
but
we do it
unwittingly.
Everything was alive,
alive, alive, alive
like a scarlet fish,
but time
passed with cloth and darkness
and kept wiping away
the flash of the fish.
Water, water, water,

the past goes on falling
although it keeps a grip
on thorns
and on roots.
It went, it went, and now
memories mean nothing.
Now the heavy eyelids
shut out the light of the eyes
and what was once alive
is now no longer living;
what we were, we are not.
And with words, although the letters
still have transparency and sound,
they change, and the mouth changes;
the same mouth is now another mouth;
they change, lips, skin, circulation;
another soul took on our skeleton;
what once was in us now is not.
It left, but if they call, we reply
''I am here,'' and we realise we are not,
that what was once, was and is lost,
lost in the past, and now does not come back.

Pablo Neruda

Goodbyes

Goodbye, goodbye, to one place or another,
to every mouth, to every sorrow,
to the insolent moon, to weeks
which wound in the days and disappeared,
goodbye to this voice and that one stained
with amaranth, and goodbye

to the usual bed and plate,
to the twilit setting of all goodbyes,
to the chair that is part of the same twilight,
to the way made by my shoes.

I spread myself, no question;
I turned over whole lives,
changed skin, lamps, and hates,
it was something I had to do,
not by law or whim,
more of a chain reaction;
each new journey enchained me;
I took pleasure in place, in all places.

And, newly arrived, I promptly said goodbye
with still newborn tenderness
as if the bread were to open and suddenly
flee from the world of the table.
So I left behind all languages,
repeated goodbyes like an old door,
changed cinemas, reasons, and tombs,
left everywhere for somewhere else;
I went on being, and being always
half undone with joy,
a bridegroom among sadnesses,
never knowing how or when,
ready to return, never returning.

It's well known that he who returns never left,
so I traced and retraced my life,
changing clothes and planets,
growing used to the company,
to the great whirl of exile,
to the great solitude of bells tolling.

Pablo Neruda

Too Many Names

Mondays are meshed with Tuesdays
and the week with the whole year.
Time cannot be cut
with your exhausted scissors,
and all the names of the day
are washed out by the waters of night.

No-one can claim the name of Pedro,
nobody is Rosa or Maria,
all of us are dust or sand,
all of us are rain under rain.
They have spoken to me of Venezuelas,
of Chiles and Paraguays;
I have no idea what they are saying.
I know only the skin of the earth
and I know it has no name.

When I lived amongst the roots
they pleased me more than flowers did,
and when I spoke to a stone
it rang like a bell.

It is so long, the spring
which goes on all winter.
Time lost its shoes.
A year lasts four centuries.

When I sleep every night,
what am I called or not called?
And when I wake, who am I
if I was not I while I slept?

This means to say that scarcely
have we landed into life
than we are as if new-born;
let us not fill our mouths
with so many faltering names,
with so many sad formalities,
with so many pompous letters,
with so much of yours and mine,
with so much signing of papers.

I have a mind to confuse things,
unite them, make them new-born,
mix them up, undress them,
until all light in the world
has the oneness of the ocean,
a generous, vast wholeness,
a crackling, living fragrance.

Pablo Neruda

Lazybones

They will continue wandering,
these things of steel among the stars,
and worn-out men will still go up
to brutalise the placid moon.
There, they will found their pharmacies.

In this time of the swollen grape,
the wine begins to come to life
between the sea and the mountain ranges.

In Chile now, cherries are dancing,
the dark, secretive girls are singing,
and in guitars, water is shining.

The sun is touching every door
and making wonder of the wheat.

The first wine is pink in colour,
is sweet with the sweetness of a child,
the second wine is able-bodied,
strong like the voice of a sailor,
the third wine is a topaz, is
a poppy and a fire in one.

My house has both the sea and the earth,
my woman has great eyes
the colour of wild hazelnut,
when night comes down, the sea
puts on a dress of white and green,
and later the moon in the spindrift foam
dreams like a sea-green girl.

I have no wish to change my planet.

Pablo Neruda

It is Born

Here I came to the very edge
where nothing at all needs saying,
everything is absorbed through weather and the sea,
and the moon swam back,
its rays all silvered,
and time and again the darkness would be broken
by the crash of a wave,
and every day on the balcony of the sea,
wings open, fire is born,
and everything is blue again like morning.

Pablo Neruda

Matthew XXV: 30

The first bridge, Constitution Station. At my feet
the shunting trains trace iron labyrinths.
Steam hisses up and up into the night,
which becomes at a stroke the night of the Last Judgment.

From the unseen horizon
and from the very centre of my being,
an infinite voice pronounced these things—
things, not words. This is my feeble translation,
time-bound, of what was a single limitless Word:

"Stars, bread, libraries of East and West,
playing-cards, chessboards, galleries, skylights, cellars,
a human body to walk with on the earth,
fingernails, growing at night-time and in death,
shadows for forgetting, mirrors busily multiplying,
cascades in music, gentlest of all time's shapes.
Borders of Brazil, Uruguay, horses and mornings,
a bronze weight, a copy of the Grettir Saga,
algebra and fire, the charge at Junin in your blood,
days more crowded than Balzac, scent of the honeysuckle,
love and the imminence of love and intolerable remembering,
dreams like buried treasure, generous luck,
and memory itself, where a glance can make men dizzy—
all this was given to you, and with it
the ancient nourishment of heroes—
treachery, defeat, humiliation.
In vain have oceans been squandered on you, in vain
the sun, wonderfully seen through Whitman's eyes.
You have used up the years and they have used up you,
and still, and still, you have not written the poem."

Jorge Luis Borges

Limits

Of all the streets that blur into the sunset,
there must be one (which, I am not sure)
that I by now have walked for the last time
without guessing it, the pawn of that Someone

who fixes in advance omnipotent laws,
sets up a secret and unwavering scale
for all the shadows, dreams, and forms
woven into the texture of this life.

If there is a limit to all things and a measure
and a last time and nothing more and forgetfulness,
who will tell us to whom in this house
we without knowing it have said farewell?

Through the dawning window night withdraws
and among the stacked books which throw
irregular shadows on the dim table,
there must be one which I will never read.

There is in the South more than one worn gate,
with its cement urns and planted cactus,
which is already forbidden to my entry,
inaccessible, as in a lithograph.

There is a door you have closed for ever
and some mirror is expecting you in vain;
to you the crossroads seem wide open,
yet watching you, four-faced, is a Janus.

There is among all your memories one
which has now been lost beyond recall.
You will not be seen going down to that fountain,
neither by white sun nor by yellow moon.

You will never recapture what the Persian
said in his language woven with birds and roses,
when, in the sunset, before the light disperses,
you wish to give words to unforgettable things.

And the steadily-flowing Rhone and the lake,
all that vast yesterday over which today I bend?
They will be as lost as Carthage,
scourged by the Romans with fire and salt.

At dawn I seem to hear the turbulent
murmur of crowds milling and fading away;
they are all I have been loved by, forgotten by;
space, time, and Borges now are leaving me.

Jorge Luis Borges

Poem of the Gifts

No one should read self-pity or reproach
into this statement of the majesty
of God, who with such splendid irony
granted me books and blindness at one touch.

Care of this city of books he handed over
to sightless eyes, which now can do no more
than read in libraries of dream the poor
and senseless paragraphs that dawns deliver

to wishful scrutiny. In vain the day
squanders on these same eyes its infinite tomes,
as distant as the inaccessible volumes
which perished once in Alexandria.

From hunger and from thirst (in the Greek story),
a king lies dying among gardens and fountains.
Aimlessly, endlessly, I trace the confines,
high and profound, of this blind library.

Cultures of East and West, the entire atlas,
encyclopedias, centuries, dynasties,
symbols, the cosmos, and cosmogonies
are offered from the walls, all to no purpose.

In shadow, with a tentative stick, I try
the hollow twilight, slow and imprecise—
I, who had always thought of Paradise
in form and image as a library.

Something, which certainly is not defined
by the word *fate*, arranges all these things;
another man was given, on other evenings
now gone, these many books. He too was blind.

Wandering through the gradual galleries,
I often feel with vague and holy dread
I am that other dead one, who attempted
the same uncertain steps on similar days.

Which of the two is setting down this poem—
a single sightless self, a plural I?
What can it matter, then, the name that names me,
given our curse is common and the same?

Groussac or Borges, now I look upon
this dear world losing shape, fading away
into a pale uncertain ashy-gray
that feels like sleep, or else oblivion.

Jorge Luis Borges

Rain

Quite suddenly the evening clears at last
as now outside the soft small rain is falling.
Falling or fallen. Rain itself is something
undoubtedly which happens in the past.

Whoever hears it falling has remembered
a time in which a curious twist of fate
brought back to him a flower whose name was ''rose''
and the perplexing redness of its red.

This rain which spreads its blind across the pane
must also brighten in forgotten suburbs
the black grapes on a vine across a shrouded

patio now no more. The evening's rain
brings me the voice, the dear voice of my father,
who comes back now, who never has been dead.

Jorge Luis Borges

Adrogué

Let no-one fear in the bewildering night
that I will lose my way among the borders
of dusky flowers that weave a cloth of symbols
appropriate to old nostalgic loves

or the sloth of afternoons—the hidden bird
forever whittling the same thin song,
the circular fountain and the summerhouse,
the indistinct statue and the hazy ruin.

Hollow in the hollow shade, the coach-house
marks (I know well) the insubstantial edges
of this particular world of dust and jasmine
so dear to Julio Herrera and Verlaine.

The shade is thick with the medicinal smell
of the eucalyptus trees, that ancient balm
which, beyond time and ambiguities
of language, brings back vanished country houses.

My step feels out and finds the anticipated
threshold. Its darkened limit is defined
by the roof, and in the chessboard patio
the water-tap drips intermittently.

On the far side of the doorways they are sleeping,
those who through the medium of dreams
watch over in the visionary shadows
all that vast yesterday and all dead things.

Each object in this venerable building
I know by heart—the flaking layers of mica
on that gray stone, reflected endlessly
in the recesses of a faded mirror,

and the lion head which holds an iron ring
in its mouth, and the multicoloured window glass,
revealing to a child the early vision
of one world coloured red, another green.

Far beyond accident and death itself
they endure, each one with its particular story,
but all this happens in the strangeness of
that fourth dimension which is memory.

In it and it alone do they exist,
the gardens and the patios. The past
retains them in that circular preserve
which at one time embraces dawn and dusk.

How could I have forgotten that precise
order of things both humble and beloved,
today as inaccessible as the roses
revealed to the first Adam in Paradise?

The ancient aura of an elegy
still haunts me when I think about that house—
I do not understand how time can pass,
I, who am time and blood and agony.

Jorge Luis Borges

Chess

I

Set in their studious corners, the players
move the gradual pieces. Until dawn
the chessboard keeps them in its strict confinement
with its two colours set at daggers drawn.

Within the game itself the forms give off
their magic rules: Homeric castle, knight
swift to attack, queen warlike, king decisive,
slanted bishop, and attacking pawns.

Eventually, when the players have withdrawn,
when time itself has finally consumed them,
the ritual certainly will not be done.

It was in the East this war took fire.
Today the whole earth is its theatre.
Like the game of love, this game goes on for ever.

Faint-hearted king, sly bishop, ruthless queen,
straightforward castle, and deceitful pawn—
over the checkered black and white terrain
they seek out and begin their armed campaign.

They do not know it is the player's hand
that dominates and guides their destiny.
They do not know an adamantine fate
controls their will and lays the battle plan.

The player too is captive of caprice
(the words are Omar's) on another ground
where black nights alternate with whiter days.

God moves the player, he in turn the piece.
But what god beyond God begins the round
of dust and time and sleep and agonies?

Jorge Luis Borges

To One No Longer Young

Already you can see the tragic setting
and each thing there in its appointed place;
the broadsword and the ash destined for Dido,
the coin prepared for Belisarius.
Why do you go on searching in the furtive
bronze of Greek hexameters for war
when these six feet of ground wait for you here,
the sudden rush of blood, the yawning grave?

Here watching you is the inscrutable glass
which will dream up and then forget the face
of all your dwindling days, your agony.
The last one now draws in. It is the house
in which your slow, brief evening comes to pass
and the street front that you look at every day.

Jorge Luis Borges

Poem Written in a Copy of Beowulf

At various times I have asked myself what reasons
moved me to study while my night came down,
without particular hope of satisfaction,
the language of the blunt-tongued Anglo-Saxons.
Used up by the years my memory
loses its grip on words that I have vainly
repeated and repeated. My life in the same way
weaves and unweaves its weary history.
Then I tell myself: it must be that the soul
has some secret sufficient way of knowing
that it is immortal, that its vast encompassing
circle can take in all, can accomplish all.
Beyond my anxiety and beyond this writing
the universe waits, inexhaustible, inviting.

Jorge Luis Borges

To My Reader

You are invulnerable. Have they not shown you,
the powers that preordain your destiny,
the certainty of dust? Is not your time
as irreversible as that same river
where Heraclitus, mirrored, saw the symbol
of fleeting life? A marble slab awaits you
which you will not read—on it, already written,
the date, the city, and the epitaph.
Other men too are only dreams of time,
not everlasting bronze nor shining gold;
the universe is, like you, a Proteus.
Dark, you will enter the darkness that expects you,
doomed to the limits of your travelled time.
Know that in some sense you by now are dead.

Jorge Luis Borges